WEEKLY WR READER

EARLY LEARNING LIBRARY

**Animals That Live
in the Mountains**

Mountain Goats

by JoAnn Early Macken

Reading consultant: Susan Nations, M.Ed.,
author/literacy coach/
consultant in literacy development

Please visit our web site at: www.garethstevens.com
For a free color catalog describing Weekly Reader® Early Learning Library's list
of high-quality books, call 1-800-542-2595 (USA) or 1-800-387-3178 (Canada).
Gareth Stevens Publishing's fax: (877) 542-2596

Library of Congress Cataloging-in-Publication Data

Macken, JoAnn Early, 1953-
    Mountain goats / by JoAnn Early Macken.
        p. cm. — (Animals that live in the mountains)
    Includes bibliographical references and index.
    ISBN-10: 0-8368-6320-8   ISBN-13: 978-0-8368-6320-8 (lib. bdg.)
    ISBN-10: 0-8368-6327-5   ISBN-13: 978-0-8368-6327-7 (softcover)
    1. Mountain goat—Juvenile literature.   I. Title.
    QL737.U53M218   2006
    599.64'75—dc22   2005028169

This edition first published in 2006 by
Weekly Reader® Early Learning Library
An Imprint of Gareth Stevens Publishing
1 Reader's Digest Rd.
Pleasantville, NY 10570-7000 USA

Managing editor: Valerie J. Weber
Art direction: Tammy West
Cover design and page layout: Kami Strunsee
Picture research: Diane Laska-Swanke

Picture credits: Cover, © Mike Anich/Visuals Unlimited; pp. 5, 9, 13, 19 © Alan & Sandy Carey;
pp. 7, 21 © Michael H. Francis; pp. 11, 15, 17 © Tom and Pat Leeson

Printed in the United States of America

2 3 4 5 6 7 8 9 10 09 08 07

Note to Educators and Parents

Reading is such an exciting adventure for young children! They are beginning to integrate their oral language skills with written language. To encourage children along the path to early literacy, books must be colorful, engaging, and interesting; they should invite the young reader to explore both the print and the pictures.

Animals That Live in the Mountains is a new series designed to help children read about creatures that make their homes in high places. Each book describes a different mountain animal's life cycle, behavior, and habitat.

Each book is specially designed to support the young reader in the reading process. The familiar topics are appealing to young children and invite them to read — and reread — again and again. The full-color photographs and enhanced text further support the student during the reading process.

In addition to serving as wonderful picture books in schools, libraries, homes, and other places where children learn to love reading, these books are specifically intended to be read within an instructional guided reading group. This small group setting allows beginning readers to work with a fluent adult model as they make meaning from the text. After children develop fluency with the text and content, the book can be read independently. Children and adults alike will find these books supportive, engaging, and fun!

— Susan Nations, M.Ed., author, literacy coach,
and consultant in literacy development

A baby mountain goat is called a **kid**. Soon after it is born, a kid can stand. It drinks milk from its mother.

In a few days, a kid starts to eat grass. For about a month, it drinks milk, too. It stays with its mother for about a year.

Kids push and chase each other. They hop off high rocks. They learn how to climb.

Male mountain goats are called **billies**. Female mountain goats are called **nannies**. Both nannies and billies grow horns and beards.

Mountain goats eat grasses and plants. They gulp down their food. Later, they bring it up and chew it again.

Mountain goats climb well.

They balance on thin ledges.

They bound down steep cliffs.

Their feet grip rocks and ice.

Nannies and kids stay in groups called **bands**. An old nanny leads each band. Billies join them in winter.

Mountain goats live high in the mountains. The weather is cold up there. Heavy coats help keep them warm in winter.

In spring, mountain goats lose their thick coats. They rub on bushes. They rub off their winter fur.

winter fur

21

Glossary

balance — to keep steady

bound — to jump

grip — to hold onto

gulp — to swallow a lot quickly

For More Information

Books

Goats. Animals That Live on the Farm (series). JoAnn Early Macken (Weekly Reader Early Learning Library)

Life on a Goat Farm. Judy Wolfman (Carolrhoda)

Mountain Goat. Zoo Animals (series). Patricia Whitehouse (Heinemann)

Mountain Goats. Frank Staub (Lerner)

Web Site

I'm a Mountain Goat
www.pbs.org/kratts/world/na/mtgoat
Mountain goat creature profile from Kratt's Creatures

Index

bands 16

beards 10

billies 10, 16

chasing 8

climbing 8, 14

coats 18, 20

feet 14

food 4, 6, 12

hopping 8

horns 10

kids 4, 6, 8

nannies 4, 6, 10, 16

pushing 8

standing 4

About the Author

JoAnn Early Macken is the author of two rhyming picture books, *Sing-Along Song* and *Cats on Judy*, and more than eighty nonfiction books for children. Her poems have appeared in several children's magazines. A graduate of the M.F.A. in Writing for Children and Young Adults Program at Vermont College, she lives in Wisconsin with her husband and their two sons.